FOOD BRANDS WE LOVE

BEN & JERRY'S

By Kaitlyn Duling

Kaleidoscope
Minneapolis, MN

The Quest for Discovery Never Ends

This edition is co-published by agreement between
Kaleidoscope and World Book, Inc.

Kaleidoscope Publishing, Inc.
6012 Blue Circle Drive
Minnetonka, MN 55343 U.S.A.

World Book, Inc.
180 North LaSalle St., Suite 900
Chicago IL 60601 U.S.A.

Kaleidoscope ISBNs
978-1-64519-208-4 (library bound)
978-1-64519-276-3 (ebook)

World Book ISBN
978-0-7166-4186-5 (library bound)

Library of Congress Control Number
2020936208

Developed and produced by Focus Strategic Communications Inc.

Printed in the United States of America.

Bigfoot lurks within one of the images in this book. It's up to you to find him!

TABLE OF
CONTENTS

Chapter 1
Mmm...Ice Cream

The day was hot. Anna was tired. She was on vacation with her parents. They were at the beach. Her forehead was sweaty. The sun beat down. She walked down the sidewalk. There were lots of shops. Suddenly, she spotted a Ben & Jerry's Scoop Shop. *Hurray*, she thought. It was a hot day, and an ice cream cone would be extra tasty. Anna pushed open the door to the shop. Her eyes widened. There were so many flavors.

FUN FACT
In 2019, the most popular Ben & Jerry's flavor was Half Baked.

Ben and Jerry's is known for the **creative** names of its ice cream flavors. The Pucker Upper flavor tastes like sour lemon and raspberry. Chocolate Therapy swirls chocolate pudding and chocolate cookies into chocolate ice cream. The Chunky Monkey flavor is filled with banana ice cream, fudge chunks, and walnuts. Anna's favorite flavor was vanilla. She pointed to the flavor. An employee scooped the ice cream into a cone.

Ben & Jerry's ice cream stores are known as Scoop Shops.

Vanilla is one of the most popular ice cream flavors.

Ice cream cones are a memorable childhood snack for many people.

Outside, Anna sat on a bench with her creamy dessert. It melted and dripped. It was cold on her tongue. The sweet treat was perfect. Anna closed her eyes and enjoyed her snack. Anna's parents each had a cone, too. They remembered Ben & Jerry's from their childhood.

The company has been in business for more than 40 years. Fans love Ben & Jerry's **values**. The company works hard to help make the world a better place. It has a mission to improve the planet while making ice cream.

FUN FACT

Historians think the first ice cream recipes were invented in the sixteenth century.

Ben & Jerry's has taken a strong stand against genetically modified organisms (GMOs) in food.

After her vacation ended, Anna was still able to get Ben & Jerry's ice cream. It is sold in grocery stores. The company also sells other products, such as cookie dough chunks. Anna would love to see how the ice cream is made. She hopes she can visit the Ben & Jerry's factory someday. For now, she is happy dreaming about her next scoop.

Simple milk with flavors and sweeteners become the miracle of ice cream.

Ben & Jerry's Ice Cream Factory is located in Waterbury, Vermont.

Chapter 2
History of Ben & Jerry's

The Ben & Jerry's company has a long history. The real Ben and Jerry are Ben Cohen and Jerry Greenfield. They grew up together on Long Island in New York. As young adults, they struggled to find success. Ben tried selling pottery. Jerry wanted to be a doctor. When those dreams did not pan out, they went into business.

At first, the two friends wanted to open a bagel shop. But the machines were expensive. Instead, they each took an ice cream making class. The class only cost five dollars. After the class, they **invested** what little money they had. They bought an old gas station in Burlington, Vermont. They fixed up the building and started making ice cream. The shop opened in 1978. Ben and Jerry were just 27 years old.

DOG DAYS

At the Ben & Jerry's office, furry friends are welcome. They are called K9-5ers. Dogs even get a daily treat. Many employees bring their dogs to work.

Ben (right) and Jerry with their modified RV, Cowmobile, in 1987.

Ben and Jerry lick ice cream cones outside their original ice cream stand in 1980.

Pints of Ben & Jerry's ice cream are a common sight in stores across the country.

Those early years were tough. Ben and Jerry tried out tons of flavors. Some, such as the first batch of Rum Raisin, did not work. Others became popular. Ice cream lovers started to flock to the Scoop Shop. By 1980, Ben and Jerry were selling pints of their ice cream to grocery stores across the country. Seven years later, their business was worth $30 million. People could grab a pint of Ben & Jerry's in 35 states.

As the years went by, Ben and Jerry dreamed up more creative flavors. Starting in the 1990s, they began to develop healthier treats, such as sorbets and low-fat ice creams. In 2016, they made another big change. They created a **vegan** ice cream. Fans loved it.

Ben & Jerry's Flavor Graveyard commemorates ice cream flavors that are no longer made.

In the year 2000, a company called Unilever bought Ben & Jerry's. However, Ben and Jerry are still involved in the company. They serve on a board of directors. They continue to make ice cream history.

FUN FACT

The average American eats more than 23 pounds (10 kg) of ice cream per year.

BEN & JERRY'S TIMELINE

1978
Ben and Jerry open their first ice cream Scoop Shop.

1979
Ben & Jerry's hosts its first Free Cone Day.

1980
Ben & Jerry's starts selling pints of ice cream to grocery stores.

1983
Ben & Jerry's ice cream is used to build the "world's largest sundae."

1991
Ben & Jerry's releases its Chocolate Chip Cookie Dough flavor. It becomes one of the most popular flavors.

1994
Stores in the United Kingdom start selling pints of Ben & Jerry's for the first time.

1995
The Ben & Jerry's website officially launches.

1978 1979 1980 1983 1991 1994 1995

2000 2002 2004 2007 2016 2018

2000
Unilever buys Ben & Jerry's.

2002
Ben & Jerry's introduces One Sweet Whirled, a flavor that raises awareness about global warming.

2004
The company partners with Rock the Vote to register voters across the United States.

2007
Ben & Jerry's organizes a protest against animal cloning at the U.S. Capitol in Washington, D.C. Protestors wear cow costumes.

2016
The first non-dairy Ben & Jerry's flavors appear on store shelves.

2018
Ben & Jerry's introduces Moo-phoria ice cream. Each flavor has fewer calories and less fat than traditional ice cream.

Chapter 3

On and Off the Farm

Sam liked eating ice cream. He wondered how it was made. He looked up the steps online. He learned that Ben & Jerry's is careful with every step of the process. It starts with the **ingredients**.

Ice cream is made with eggs and milk. The eggs are cage-free. The chickens have plenty of space to move and walk. They also have lots of food and water. The milk comes from cows that are treated well. Ben and Jerry believe that animals deserve to live happy lives.

Ben & Jerry's was one of the first companies to promote cage-free eggs.

Ben & Jerry's created the Caring Dairy program to encourage farmers to provide better care for their cows.

FUN FACT

There are 577 Ben & Jerry's shops across the globe.

Ben & Jerry's only uses products, such as coffee beans, that are fair trade.

Coffee, vanilla, chocolate, and bananas are grown around the world. Some farmers outside the United States do not earn much money. Sam learned that Ben & Jerry's partners with **fair trade** farms and co-ops. In fair trade programs, farmers get paid a fair wage.

Sam's parents like that Ben & Jerry's is vocal about politics. The company leads protests. It raises money for causes. It designs its pints to reflect the company's values. In 2015, Ben & Jerry's released a flavor call I Dough, I Dough. It showed support

Same-sex marriage is one of many progressive issues the company supports.

for marriage equality. In 2016, Ben and Jerry got arrested at the U.S. Capitol. They were protesting for voter rights.

In 2019, Ben & Jerry's announced the flavor Justice Remix'd to highlight racism in the justice system.

FUN FACT

In 2019, Ben & Jerry's made a new flavor called Justice Remix'd. It calls attention to racism in the United States.

Ben & Jerry's reach is worldwide. But the company also focuses on the local level. It donates money to nonprofits. It supports groups in Vermont and across the country. Sam's family lives in Vermont. They like it when businesses help out.

ICE CREAM RECYCLING

When ice cream is produced, waste is made. The waste cannot be eaten. Usually, it is thrown away. But Ben & Jerry's sends their dairy waste back to dairy farms. There, it is put into a machine. The machine makes energy. That energy powers the farms.

In 2008, Ben & Jerry's launched the Ice Cream Social Movement to fight global poverty.

Chapter 4
Ice Cream Fanatics

Kiya loves ice cream. She loves Ben & Jerry's ice cream the most. One of the things fans love most about the Ben & Jerry's brands is the flavor options. Some flavors are only sold in certain countries.

In Japan, there is a sweet potato flavor. The sweet potatoes are purple. There is also a passion fruit flavor in Japan. One Canadian flavor is full of ingredients. It features toffee, peanut butter cups, and almonds. In some parts of Europe, Ben & Jerry's offers a banana ice cream. It is dotted with cookie swirls and chocolate peace signs.

Favorite ice cream flavors include Baked Alaska, Peanut Butter Cup, and Pistachio Pistachio.

Ben & Jerry's shops differ from country to country.

Vegan non-dairy flavors are made with sunflower butter or almond milk.

Kiya's brother is vegan. He does not eat ice cream. But in 2016, Ben & Jerry's revealed vegan treats. Their non-dairy flavors are not made with cow's milk. Instead, they are made with almond milk. This is important for vegans. It also helps those who are **lactose intolerant**. Kiya's brother was excited. Kiya liked the vegan flavors, too.

Kiya's dad eats the light version of Ben & Jerry's ice cream. It has less fat and sugar. Frozen yogurt is also low in fat. In 2017, the company created Pint Slices. These are disks of ice cream covered in chocolate.

BEN & JERRY'S TOP 10

1. **Half Baked** Chocolate, Vanilla, & Fudge Brownie
2. **Cherry Garcia** Cherry & Fudge
3. **The Tonight Dough** Caramel & Chocolate with Peanut Butter
4. **Chocolate Chip Cookie Dough** Vanilla with Chocolate
5. **Chocolate Fudge Brownie** Chocolate & Fudge
6. **Phish Food** Chocolate with Marshmallow, Caramel, & Fudge
7. **Strawberry Cheesecake** Strawberry
8. **Americone Dream** Vanilla with Fudge & Caramel
9. **Mint Chocolate Cookie** Peppermint with Chocolate
10. **Milk & Cookies** Vanilla with Chocolate Chip Cookies

Long lines at Ben & Jerry's San Francisco location show how popular their ice cream is.

Cow statues are outside the Ben & Jerry's ice cream factory in Vermont.

Kiya's family is crazy about Ben & Jerry's. So are fans around the world. From the fun flavor names to vegan options, there is something for everyone. For more than 40 years, the company has created new treats. Fans cannot wait to see what the next 40 years will bring.

THE BEST DAY EVER

Every year, Ben & Jerry's hosts Free Cone Day. It has been a tradition since 1979. On that day, each customer gets a free ice cream cone. There are no rules. Fans can get in line as many times as they want! Of course, they have to be willing to wait for their order.

BEYOND THE BOOK

After reading the book, it's time to think about what you learned. Try the following exercises to jumpstart your ideas.

THINK

THAT'S NEWS TO ME. Ben & Jerry's is involved in many social and political issues. The company makes statements. It holds protests. Consider how you learn about events and issues. What information can be found in news articles? What about news programs on TV? Where can you go to find news you can trust?

CREATE

PRIMARY SOURCES. Primary sources provide firsthand accounts of an event. Interviews, videos, and photographs are all examples of primary sources. Create a list of the kinds of primary sources you might be able to find about Ben & Jerry's.

SHARE

WHAT'S YOUR OPINION? The text states that Ben & Jerry's takes its ice cream seriously. Do you agree with that statement? Provide evidence from the text to support your opinion. Share your position and evidence with a friend. Does your friend find the argument convincing?

GROW

DRAWING CONNECTIONS. Create a diagram that shows and explains connections between Ben & Jerry's and its ingredient suppliers. How does learning about ingredients help you better understand Ben & Jerry's?

RESEARCH NINJA

Visit www.ninjaresearcher.com/2084 to learn how to take your research skills and book report writing to the next level!

RESEARCH

DIGITAL LITERACY TOOLS

SEARCH LIKE A PRO

Learn how to use search engines to find useful websites.

FACT OR FAKE?

Discover how you can tell a trusted website from an untrustworthy resource.

TEXT DETECTIVE

Explore how to zero in on the information you need most.

SHOW YOUR WORK

Research responsibly—learn how to cite sources.

WRITE

GET TO THE POINT

Learn how to express your main ideas.

PLAN OF ATTACK

Learn prewriting exercises and create an outline.

DOWNLOADABLE REPORT FORMS

Further Resources

BOOKS

Bader, Bonnie. *Curious About Ice Cream*. London, UK: Penguin Young Readers, 2017.

Leaf, Christina. *Ice Cream*. Hopkins, MN: Bellwether Media, 2020.

Miller, Derek. *The Making of Everyday Things: Ice Cream*. New York, NY: Cavendish Square, 2019.

Schloss, Andrew. *Amazing (Mostly) Edible Science: A Family Guide to Fun Experiments in the Kitchen*. Beverly, MA: Quarry Books, 2016.

WEBSITES

FACTSURFER

Factsurfer.com gives you a safe, fun way to find more information.

1. Go to www.factsurfer.com.
2. Enter "Ben & Jerry's" into the search box and click
3. Select your book cover to see a list of related websites.

Glossary

creative: To use new and original ideas.

fair trade: An arrangement in which producers in developing countries and companies in developed countries negotiate fair prices and improved social standards.

ingredients: Parts or elements of a recipe.

invested: The act of putting money into something in the hope of making a profit.

lactose intolerant: Unable to digest lactose, a component of dairy products.

values: Principles or standards.

vegan: Products or people that do not use animal products.

Index

PHOTO CREDITS

The images in this book are reproduced through the courtesy of: Keith Homan/Shutterstock Images, front cover (Ben & Jerry's ice cream products), pp. 1, 4, 14 (top right), 15 (top), 22 (Peanut Butter Cup & Pistachio, Pistachio), 31; Dudarev Mikhail/Shutterstock Images, front cover (cow); Nikos Andreou/Shutterstock Images, front cover (scoop of ice cream), p. 3; foxaon1987/Shutterstock Images, p. 1 (background); enchanted_fairy/Shutterstock Images, p. 5 (top); Bananastory/Shutterstock Images, p. 5 (bottom); Dmitry Lobanov/Shutterstock Images, p. 6; Steve Jennings/Getty Images, p. 7; ASA studio/Shutterstock Images, p. 8; Jay Yuan/Shutterstock Images, pp. 8-9; Susan Schmitz/Shutterstock Images, p. 10; Toby Talbot/AP Images, p. 11 (top); Ted Dully/Boston Globe/Getty Images, p. 11 (bottom); Anne Beruldsen/Shutterstock Images, p. 12; karenfoleyphotography/Shutterstock Images, p. 13 (top); ChameleonsEye/Shutterstock Images, p. 13 (bottom); makesushi1/Shutterstock Images, p. 14 (top left); M. Unal Ozmen/Shutterstock Images, pp. 14 (bottom), 27 (bottom left); Martin Kovacik/Shutterstock, pp. 15 (bottom), 24; spiro/Shutterstock Images, p. 16; Guitar photographer/Shutterstock Images, pp. 16-17; Brastock/Shutterstock Images, p. 18; Anthony Upton/PA Wire URN:17062352/AP Images, p. 19 (top); Win McNamee/Getty Images, p. 19 (bottom); AlessandroZocc/Shutterstock Images, p. 20; Kevork Djansezian/AP Images, pp. 20-21; Lenscap Photography/Shutterstock Images, p. 22 (Baked Alaska); Tommy Larey/Shutterstock Images, p. 23 (top); Cromo Digital/Shutterstock Images, p. 23 (bottom); Israel Mckee/Shutterstock Images, p. 25; tupungato/iStockphoto, p. 26; Wangkun Jia/Shutterstock Images, p. 27 (center right).

About the Author

Kaitlyn Duling loves ice cream, especially chocolate. She lives in Washington, D.C.